Praise for

Mark and Jacquelyn bring practice ways to build a Kingdom business. Work really is worship because it is a redemptive process. This book will encourage you to leave a legacy in the marketplace.

Glenn Repple, Founder and President
G.A. Repple Financial Group

Mark Goldstein's thoughts in *Work as Worship* are an authentic account and a gift of wisdom tempered by experience, smarts, and good humor. Having walked alongside Mark as the Chairman of the Board of the Central Florida Chamber, I've been privy to his behind-the-scenes thinking and conversations. In the end, Mark always presses into what would best build the Kingdom of God and honor God.

Kevin W. McCarthy, Author, The On-Purpose Person
Chief Leadership Officer, On-Purpose Partners

Work as Worship skillfully captures the man, his faith, message, and life. To all who desire meaningful impact in life and career, Mark Goldstein's insight, experience. and advice is now readily available. As Mark often says, "Keep building!"

Bill Snell, President
Missionary Ventures International

Mark Goldstein has a heart for the Lord that is unmistakable. He is uniquely qualified to talk about work as worship because he lives it out daily. *Work as Worship* is filled with excellent advice and encouragement. Most importantly, it clearly reflects Mark's heart to glorify his Father in Heaven. I highly recommend you read it.

Kris DenBesten
author of Shine, The Shine Factor, *and* Gracyn's Song
CEO, Vermeer Southeast

Wow! What a wide-ranging and comprehensive overview of the topic of work as worship. Mark Goldstein is one of the most sincere and knowledgeable Christian leaders I have met in Central Florida. In the ten years I have had the joy of knowing Mark, he has helped me with challenges that I faced in my work at Asbury Seminary many times. In *Work As Worship* Mark clearly articulates a way for all of us that serve in the business community and respond to God's call in our lives as we seek to serve him in our endeavors.

Bill Tillmann, Development Officer
Asbury Seminary

Work as Worship is an easy-to-read reminder that my work is my ministry. Mark does an excellent job of sharing a roadmap that anyone can follow to take their faith into the workplace and leave a legacy.

Heath Ritenour, Chairman & CEO
Insurance Office of America

Thank you, Jacquelyn, for putting this excellent book together. Thank you, Mark, for sharing your great wisdom with authenticity. No matter how long you have had a relationship with God, this book will inspire and challenge you to make every moment of every day count for the specific purpose and the destiny God has for all of us. The title of the book is perfect for the rich content and guidance it provides. No matter your work situation (outside home or at home), you will be blessed and encouraged by *Work as Worship*. Well done, Jacquelyn and Mark.

Pete Folch, Founder/President
Second Wind-Finish Strong, Inc.

"What are you doing here?" Mark Goldstein turns five common words into profound meaning and beautifully illuminates the importance of living out our faith in our workplace.

Stephanie Nelson Garris, Chief Executive Officer
Grace Medical Home

I've known Mark Goldstein for seven years. He's the real deal, and so his is message about marketplace ministry. Mark combines his faith, his marketplace ministry expertise, and his real-life formula for turning your business or career into a legacy. I highly recommend *Work as Worship*.

Rich Panner, VP Sales
Pepsico Beverages North America

Mark Goldstein provides a wealth of valuable information for those of us looking to leave a legacy of faith in the workplace. As a young professional with decades of work ahead of me, Mark's ministry-focused reminders are encouraging calls to action. *Work as Worship* combines Mark's experiences with his natural likability and charm to present a treasure trove of work-related Biblical truth.

Michael Strawser, Principal
Legacy Communication Training and Consulting

For years I struggled to feel at peace about my work. At times, I thought my work was too much of who I was. Other times, I struggled to find the right combination of work and faith. In *Work as Worship*, Mark accomplishes in writing what he has done for years: help people like me to understand that work is what we *do* and not who we *are*, and that we are called to do our best and then rest. I recommend this book to all believers who are struggling at times at work because it will help you find peace and purpose.

John Crossman, CCIM, CRX
CEO, Crossman Career Builders

Mark Goldstein demonstrates not only his intense knowledge of the concept of work as worship, but his heart and passion for seeing people being fulfilled in Christ to impact their world, work, and the Kingdom. *Work as Worship* should be required reading for all Christian businesses, pastors, and laypeople no matter the field they find themselves in.

Jeff A Yant, Executive Director / CEO
Lake Yale Baptist Conference Center

What a valuable read! Jacquelyn Lynn and Mark Goldstein do a tremendous job of providing practical thoughts for carrying Christianity into the work field. Discussion of how performed work should reflect Christian principles is thoughtful and useful. Careful study of *Work as Worship* will be of immense help to anyone interested in combining Biblical and business principles to enhance personal and organizational success. Do yourself a favor—get it now!

Dr. Samuel C. Certo, Emeritus Dean and Professor of Management
Rollins College MBA Program

What an excellent way to spend an afternoon! *Work as Worship* is loaded with relevance and reminders. Having known Mark a few years now, his genuine, compassionate, voice comes right through the pages. A few times it felt like Mark was speaking directly with me. Perfect timing. Through her questions, Jacquelyn Lynn did a marvelous job incorporating Mark's Biblical wisdom with his down-to-earth, practical nature. This little book will feed your soul, challenge you, and give you just the right 'nudge' to help you remember to be the light.

Karen Pelot, CEO
Perspectives, LLC

How often do we ever get to really sit down with a demonstrated expert in marketplace ministry? In this book, Jacquelyn Lynn and Mark Goldstein take you on a journey of revelation, encouragement, and practical hands-on insights that will move you to another level of understanding and fruitfulness.

Peter Lowe, CEO
Elev8 Christian Business Summits

Work

as

Worship

Conversations

IDEAS
INFORMATION

Experts share their knowledge and experience

Work
as
Worship

How Your Labor Becomes Your Legacy

An interview with marketplace ministry expert Mark Goldstein

Jacquelyn Lynn

Tuscawilla Creative Services, LLC
Goldenrod, FL USA
CreateTeachInspire.com

For bulk orders, contact info@contacttcs.com

This publication is designed to provide accurate and authoritative information regarding the subject matter covered. It is sold with the understanding that the publisher and author are not engaged in rendering legal, accounting or other professional services. If legal advice or other expert assistance is required, the services of a competent professional should be sought.

Library of Congress Control Number: 2020907526

ISBN Paperback: 978-1-941826-35-5
ISBN Ebook: 978-1-941826-36-2

He told them, "The harvest is plentiful, but the workers are few. Ask the Lord of the harvest, therefore, to send out workers into his harvest field.

Luke 10:2 (NIV)

Contents

Introduction

Being a person of faith—any faith—has never been easy. Religious persecution has existed throughout human history. In modern times, rarely a day goes by that we don't hear about a Christian business being targeted for operating according to Biblical principles. But as important as that issue is, it's not the focus of this book.

The more compelling message of living as a person of faith centers on the eternal results of how we invest our life on Earth. Once we reach adulthood and get out of school, most of us spend more than a third of our time working. Beyond the mechanics of our jobs, what are we accomplishing? Are we merely putting in the necessary hours until we can get away from the office or the factory to do something else? Or are we using our labor to create a legacy that will reflect our faith far beyond our immediate reach now and for generations to come?

The key to creating that legacy is to make our work an act of worship. And it's easier than you might think. Whether you're a rank-and-file employee, a corporate executive, or a business owner, you can leave an indelible imprint on the world through your work.

When I first had the idea to ask Mark Goldstein to sit down with me for a Conversations talk, I thought we'd discuss marketing. After all, the man is a veritable factory of marketing ideas, and he's passionate about helping others succeed by developing and implementing creative marketing strategies. I've included his biography at the end of this book so you can see his credentials.

> Very truly I tell you, whoever believes in me will do the works I have been doing, and they will do even greater things than these, because I am going to the Father.
>
> *John 14:12 (NIV)*

With his experience, we could cover so many aspects of marketing that would help you grow your business. As I was thinking about how to narrow down the focus, I heard Mark give a speech on marketplace ministry. It was an incredible eye-opener for me, and I knew immediately this was the message that needed to be shared.

Mark agreed. Over several sessions, we talked at length about the challenges Christians face in the workplace and—more importantly—how to turn your particular workplace into a marketplace ministry that will let you serve in ways you never imagined.

Work as Worship is an edited transcript of my conversation with Mark Goldstein about how you can turn your labor into your legacy while practicing marketplace ministry in today's complex business landscape.

Jacquelyn Lynn

Chapter One

Faith in the Workplace

Jacquelyn Lynn: What is the biggest challenge facing Christians in the workplace?

Mark Goldstein: It's related to a word we hear a lot that's sometimes overused: purpose. There's so much talk about finding out what your purpose is. Why am I here? What do I need to do? What happens when I get older—what do I do then? But we're focusing on the temporal. We're trying to define our purpose by our jobs, by our families, by our standing in the community, by our hobbies.

I think our biggest challenge comes from the fact that we're not asking God to reveal his purpose for us.

He knew us before we were in the womb. He made us. He created us for excellence. What did he have in mind when he put Mrs. Goldstein's egg with Mr. Goldstein's sperm? What did he have in mind for little Mark? This is what we need to ask; this is what we need to find out.

We serve a loving God who gives us a talent, a skill set, a passion set, and he winds us up and says, "Go and do, go and have fun." So I think our biggest challenge is understanding that he has equipped us to go and do something for him for eternity.

JL: So the challenge is not that we're trying to figure out our purpose but that we're being distracted by worldly things in the process?

MG: Right. Do we identify our purpose as that place where we do business? Certainly, we can use our businesses as a platform. But is there a purpose that's not necessarily seen on the surface? That's not readily apparent? I believe there is.

We are so busy just trying to survive. We have responsibilities, we have bills to pay, we have all this stuff going on—it's like Maslow's hierarchy of needs. Everybody wants to self-actualize, but we first have to deal with the basic needs of survival. Too many people are focused on figuring out how to survive, rather than asking, "How do I thrive?" And the way we thrive is when we know and live God's purpose for us.

> "At the heart of working men and women is the longing—though oft forgotten and sadly despaired of—to participate in something greater than themselves, to belong to a cause that is meaningful and to share in a legacy that endures."
> Richard D. Phillips
> *The Heart of an Executive: Lessons on Leadership from the Life of King David*

JL: I want to ask you about how we know God's purpose for us, but first, let's talk about how Christians can take their faith into the workplace in today's environment that is so divisive and volatile. We hear stories daily about the cancel culture—meaning that if someone has an opinion the crowd doesn't share, or does something the crowd finds objectionable, that person is canceled, boycotted, fired, driven out of business. Companies like Chick-fil-A and Hobby Lobby are regular targets. Individual Christians have been attacked for their personal opinions, for the organizations or political candidates they support. It's understandable that some people feel the safest approach could be to stay quiet about their faith.

MG: I think it comes down to you have to be true to yourself. You have to be true to your own DNA. You have to be comfortable in your own skin.

We've all heard the quote usually attributed to St. Francis of Assisi that we should all be ready to preach the gospel at all times and when necessary use words. That's true.

Christianity is not *what* we are but *who* we are. Having faith means having integrity, it means being honest. If you say you are going to do something, do it. Be true to your word. Do the right thing even when it doesn't seem beneficial to you. We attract people not by what we say but by who they perceive we are—by what we do.

As far as work as worship goes, consider that we spend the lion's share of our week in the marketplace, doing our jobs.

Of course, you have people who work in the home and they never see anybody or—God bless them—moms and even dads whose career is raising the kids. But for the vast majority of folks, we are in the marketplace a minimum of 40 hours a week. Nowadays the new normal is about 60 hours a week. That's a lot of hours.

Now, we have some hours sleeping, we have some hours being at home, we have some hours at church and play, but the lion's share of our week is in the marketplace. So who are we in the marketplace?

If we have a relationship with the Lord, that relationship

goes two ways, and everything that we do is a process of how strong that relationship is.

When I have the honor and privilege of engaging with individuals in my work, it's an honor and privilege because, through those interactions, I get to reflect Jesus in the marketplace. To me, that's worship. The whole idea of work as worship is: Does what you do reflect who God is?

JL: When I was younger, I had a series of jobs—most that I enjoyed, a few not so much. But they were jobs. I went to work and did them. To me, worship was something people did on Sundays in church. If you had suggested to me then that work could be worship, I would have thought you were nuts. I'm sure a lot of people would agree with me even today. How can work possibly be worship?

MG: Go back to the Garden of Eden. Adam didn't sit around smelling the flowers and looking at the pretty sky and watching all the nice little critters run around. He had a job, and the job was naming those animals. By naming them, he was in a relationship with God. God gave him a responsibility; Adam accepted the responsibility.

For us, when God gives us skills, an acumen of sorts, and we express ourselves with that acumen and skill, we are, in essence, giving back to him in relationship with what he has given us. It's that outward working of relationship that's acknowledging who he is and who we are and the blessing we have in doing what we do—that's worship.

Honoring God through what I do and what I say, how I interact with people—that comes down to worship.

JL: And to honor God, you don't even have to say his name.

MG: No, not at all. It's more effective when you don't, I think.

JL: *When we talk about work as worship, we need to distinguish between two key things. One, doing your work as a form of worship in that you are using the skills and gifts that God gave you and giving them back to him and, two, actually worshiping the work you do. We are not saying you are to worship work.*

MG: Right.

JL: *Along with that is that it's so easy to look at work as drudgery, as just stuff you have to get done. It might be manual labor, it might be a high-level report, but it's work you have to do. How can you look at that as worship?*

MG: By looking at the end game. What are the results, what is being accomplished by this? Whether you are digging a ditch, putting on a roof, doing somebody's taxes, working on an assembly line—what is the end result? Maybe you are doing the same thing over and over, and you wonder why you're doing it, you're bored, you don't enjoy it. But look beyond the one thing that you're doing. How is that integral in the end product that goes out the door or the end service that's provided to the customer? If you don't do your job with excellence, what will the end product not be able to do? And if it does what it's supposed to do, how does the end-user benefit?

Let's say you're working in a motorcycle factory on the assembly line, doing the same thing over and over, day in, day out. A motorcycle you worked on goes out onto the market. It's sold and given to somebody who is in the mission field. Because of that motorcycle, because it was built with quality and accuracy, instead of getting to one church, a pastor can get to five churches every week. If work is worship for you, what you do has eternal impact.

It's the idea of being, as Paul tells Titus in the King James Version, a peculiar person.

> *Who gave himself for us, that he might redeem us*
> *from all iniquity, and purify unto himself a peculiar*
> *people, zealous of good works. (Titus 2:14, KJV)*

We know that doesn't mean we are to be odd. But in a world of chaos when we are at peace, and in a world of cold when we are warm, and in a world of hate when we are loving, and in a world of "I don't care" and indifference when we care, it sets us apart. We are that fish swimming upstream.

People look at us and they say, "Wow, that's different." That's what I think being salt and light is—the light we are reflecting and the salt we are infusing. You know salt was used as a preservative, so if we are infusing our Christian values in the marketplace, there is some preserving there. We are preserving, not by what we say but by who we are.

JL: So you're saying that we need to look at the marketplace as a ministry field.

MG: Absolutely.

Chapter Two

The Marketplace as a Ministry Field

Jacquelyn Lynn: What does seeing the marketplace as a ministry field mean, and why is that important to Christians?

Mark Goldstein: There's a story about Elijah in 1 Kings 18-19 that we can learn from. Elijah was called to do some work. The work was to confront Ahab, the king, and Jezebel, his wife—actually Jezebel was really the king because Ahab acquiesced to her all the time. But back to the story: Elijah finally said to Ahab, "Listen, get all the prophets, bring them together, and we are going to have the showdown at Mount Carmel. We are going to bring this to a conclusion."

Then Elijah said to the people, "Listen, if God is God, serve him. If Baal is God, serve him."

And the people said, "Fine, let's do it."

We know the prophets built an altar, and throughout the whole day, they were calling on Baal to take the sacrifice, and he doesn't. Finally, Elijah—in something that would make for a really good movie, dramatic and theatrical—rebuilds a proper altar with twelve stones from the tribes of Israel. He cuts the animal and puts the sacrifice in and says, "Okay, pour water on it," and they did. Then he says, "Do it again," and they do it again. "Do it again," and they do it again.

There was a river of water in a trench around the altar, and Elijah called on God, who lapped it all up. The people kill the prophets of Baal, and it looked like an amazing work that Elijah did. But then Jezebel said, "If you are alive this time tomorrow, God needs to punish me. I am going to kill you."

Elijah was doing his work, and he ran. He didn't just run, he ran 40 days, and he went from Mount Carmel to Mount Horeb. It was like he was running home to daddy because Mount Horeb was Mount Sinai where the Ten Commandments were given. He gets there in 40 days, completely off his purpose, completely off what God had called him to do.

It was much like what Peter did when he said to Jesus, "Let me walk to you," and Jesus said, "Come on." Peter got out of the boat and was walking until he took his eyes off Jesus and realized that he was walking on water and that nobody has ever walked on water, and he started going down.

> "Not really knowing how to handle the delicate subject of God in a secular setting, particularly with senior people in the business world, I telephoned John Gardner and told him of my uncertainty about how to respond. John simply said, 'Over the entrance to Carl Jung's home is a Latin inscription *Vocatus atque non vocatus, Deus aderit*— Invoked or not invoked, God is present.'"
>
> Joseph Jaworski
> *Synchronicity: The Inner Path of Leadership*

Elijah took his eyes off the ball. He got discouraged, and he ran. He got to Mount Horeb, and God met him there. God didn't get on Elijah's case. God didn't scold him, didn't chastise him. He just asked Elijah a simple question.

"Elijah, what are you doing here?"

I believe that God asking Elijah, "What are you doing here?" is the key for us to understand marketplace ministry.

JL: I'm not getting that. Can you make a connection for me?

MG: I think that the question was really asked in three ways:

Elijah, what are <u>you</u> doing here?

Elijah, what are you <u>doing</u> here?

And finally,

Elijah, what are you doing <u>here</u>?

I think that cut Elijah to the bone. We know from the subsequent story that after Elijah answered God, he was refocused and once again very effective in the marketplace in his ministry.

Chapter Three

What are <u>You</u> Doing Here?

Jacquelyn Lynn: Okay, let's take that apart. What are <u>you</u> doing here? Let's talk about <u>you</u> in this context.

MG: The simple answer is that we—the <u>you</u>—are God's children. God's heirs. And he loves us more than any human parent has ever loved a child. Regardless of a person's denomination, regardless of how they interpret and how they engage in their faith, the bottom line that cuts across any denomination or non-denomination is the fact that God is absolutely, positively head over heels in love with each one of us. It's undeniable. He loves us so much.

In the first chapter of 1 Peter, Peter talks about where his inheritance—where God's sons' and daughters' inheritance—where all of those good things that we will have for all of eternity is sitting in safekeeping. He talks about what Heaven looks like, wherever it is, and whatever abode we're going to have.

But it's waiting for us. Why don't we have it right now? Because it's like anything else—we'd bugger it up. We're not ready for it. But we are his sons and daughters. We are loved by him. Even when we goof up.

Those of us who are parents understand this. Our kids do things wrong. Sometimes they do terrible things. But do we ever stop loving them?

JL: No. We may not always like them, but we never stop loving them.

MG: Right. We don't like some of the things they do, but we never pull our love away. Loving parents discipline their children. God does that to us.

In Genesis 3, when Adam and Eve sinned, God came and walked through Eden in the cool of the day, and he asked a question: "Where are you?"

Not, "What are you doing?" but "Where are you?" He didn't need to ask that. He knew where they were, and he knew what they were doing. And he had a plan to redeem them.

Something else this story illustrates is that Christianity is the only religion where God comes to man. Right from the very beginning, he came to Adam and Eve.

Throughout the Old Testament, you read about a God who has so much patience with stubborn people and people who continually turn their backs on him, who continually spit in his face, if you will. And he never stopped loving them.

Over and over he would say, "Here are the blessings, here are the curses. But even with the curses, I will redeem you. I can't stop loving you. I can't let you go." And throughout the entire Old Testament, it's God willing his kids, saying, "I'm here. I love you. Love me back."

How do we love back? Through relationship. God told

them, "Don't rely on Baal, don't rely on this and that. Just trust me."

Over and over, they disobeyed, until finally, the answer was, "I am going to give my life for you. I am going to sacrifice myself for you. To show once and for all, you are mine. And all I am asking you to do is accept."

We often talk about justice. That's not justice. Justice is we should have gotten what we deserve instead of God taking on what he didn't deserve.

You know, it blows me away, but that's the God that we serve. To realize that we may run from him, but he never runs from us. And the same God who would go to the cross and suffer what he did, how much more will he go to the wall to save us? To keep us?

If that's what he did to save us, what will he do now to give us everything we need to serve him? To give us all the tools, the skills, the passion—everything we need?

JL: So we just have to be receptive?

MG: Yes, and that comes back to worship. He gives, we receive. We give, he receives. He receives our praise, our adoration, not in lip service, but in tangible actions.

We are God's children. God is our king. That makes us royalty. When we understand who we are, that we are royalty—I mean, we read about the royals these days and all the soap opera drama with them. But the reality is, *we* are the royalty. And we have a relationship with our king.

Let's talk about relationships. Think about what we read about Jesus. We read about when he was a baby. We read about when he was 12, and then the scripture is silent for about 18 years until he was confronted by John the Baptist.

What happened during those 18 years?

Though the Bible is silent, history is not. We know that in Biblical days when a young boy was seen to have the talent, the acumen, he was chosen by the rabbis. An early part of boys' educations was to memorize the Torah. Those who did it well were chosen by the rabbis to go on to memorize the rest of the scripture. Those who were the best of the best were then called by the rabbi.

That's what's so amazing about the disciples. They did not cut the mustard. They had to go back to their parents' businesses, so Jesus chose those who were not the best of the best.

But back to how young Jewish boys were educated. We know that the boys who showed the most promise were chosen to sit under the tutelage of a rabbi like Paul sat under the tutelage of Gamaliel.

We don't read about Jesus sitting under the tutelage of a rabbi, but clearly, when he was in the temple when he was 12, they were astounded—not by his answers, but by his questions. He would ask questions which were so insightful it was clear that he should have been under the tutelage of a rabbi, but he wasn't.

Or was he?

As far as we can tell, he wasn't being taught by a human rabbi, but I believe he was under the tutelage of a rabbi—his Father.

John 1:1, 14 says, "In the beginning was the Word, and the Word was with God, and the Word was God. ... And the Word was made flesh, and dwelt among us." Jesus is the Word. He is the Name above all names. He is God in the flesh.

Jesus knew who he was because of his relationship with the Father and the Father breathing his Word into him. Jesus read the scriptures. Jesus knew his calling. He knew his mission. He knew this when he was in his teens. He knew about Golgotha, and he did it.

The point to all of this is that I believe Jesus knew himself by spending time with the Father and scripture. That's the way we get to know Jesus. The way we get to know the Father is by spending time with him in scripture.

JL: And in that process, we are also getting to know who we are.

MG: Jesus knew who he was because he read about himself in the scriptures. We have the blessing of having not only up to Malachi, we have the rest of it. Like Paul Harvey would say, we have the rest of the story. We see Jesus in his fullness. We see what angels saw. But to understand who we are and the blessing, the privilege, the honor, the responsibility of who we are—and not only who we are, but our mission, our whole reason for being—we get that through spending time with the Father.

I went to Bible school and studied like you're supposed to study, but I never read through the Bible from cover to cover. In early 2013, I got my first smartphone. I sent out an email to a bunch of friends, and I said, "I just got my smartphone. I don't know one app from another. What do you recommend?"

Almost nine out of ten people said the YouVersion Bible app. So I downloaded it and started looking through it, and I saw that there were different reading and study plans. Under the whole Bible, it said, "Bible in 90 days." I thought, you've got to be kidding me. I can't do that. Nobody can read the Bible in 90 days.

So to prove that nobody can read the Bible in 90 days, I started the plan. Well, 45 days in, I was still on track. I thought to myself, I can do this. I can keep going. It's like the guy who is swimming across the English Channel. He gets halfway, and he's tired, but what's the point in going back? So at that point, I decided that rather than proving I couldn't do this, I would prove that I could. And I did.

It didn't take me long to figure out that if you could read the Bible in 90 days, you could do it four times a year. So that was my next goal. Since I began this journey in February 2013, as of today, when we are doing this interview, I am on day 25 for my thirty-second time. And you know what? It keeps getting better every time.

But I don't do it as a Bible study. I do it as somebody would want to read a novel. I do it like reading your book *Choices*. I do it for pleasure. I do it for insight. I do it just to let it speak to me. That's how I read the Bible. I just let the Holy Spirit speak to me. And I am finding that I am averaging completing it in about 70-75 days because there are some days I just don't want to stop. Take Acts, for example. I read Acts from start to finish to really get the breadth of it.

> "It is important to keep a still place in the 'marketplace.' This still place is where God can dwell and speak to us. It is also the place from which we can speak in a healing way to all the people we meet in our busy days. Without that still place we start spinning."
>
> Henri J.M. Nouwen
> *Bread for the Journey*

But here is the beauty: Genesis 1:1 says, "In the beginning, God created the heaven and the earth." At the end, in Revelation 21, John wrote, "And I saw a new heaven and a new earth." Everything in between is the greatest love story you could ever, ever read. And to realize that the story is for me. The story is meant to speak to me.

So do I have bad days? Sure. Do I have good days? Sure. But I always have wonderful days because every day God gives me something for that day. It's like the widow woman from Zarephath that Elijah met. She was almost out of food. Elijah asked her for something to eat, and she said, "I have to make a meal for my son and me, and then we are going to die." But God had told Elijah that she would sustain him, so he said, "Well, make a little cake for me first, then make something for yourself." And every day until the drought was over, she tipped the barrel, and there was food for the day. [1 Kings 17]

Every day through the Bible, God gives me something. What's wonderful is that I do not need a commentary to get it. Of course, there are times when I do research to find out more, but I find that scripture explains scripture. The dots get connected.

JL: I feel like we're digressing from the you question, but let me ask one last question about reading the Bible before we move on. You've told me before that it's important to take the time to study scripture, and you have an approach to it that I think is different from a lot of people. I think many people look at Bible study almost in the same way they look at homework from school. It's just one more thing we have to do, and we're busy. You've pointed out a different angle—that reading and studying the Bible is not a chore. But to read the entire Bible in 90 days—I can hear our readers saying, "I don't have time. God will understand that I'm busy, I have a business to run, I have a family to take care of, I'm doing all this stuff, and I'm serving my church and my community. I don't have time to read the Bible in 90 days." What do you say to those people?

MG: You can't afford not to have time. Could you imagine a husband and wife—they're married, but they sleep in separate bedrooms. When they greet each other in the morning, they wave at each other, leave and go their separate ways, come home at night, fix their own dinner, read the paper, watch TV and maybe they say goodnight and then head to their separate bedrooms. Is that a marriage? Is that a relationship?

JL: No.

MG: That's the way some people treat God. He's there, but he's not. I mean, how can you have a relationship with somebody and not spend time with them? Not share your feelings and not hear theirs? Not be there for each other and not nurture and uplift each other? I know this example is hyperbole, but it makes the point. And then you have people who respond to that by saying, okay, I'll do the homework. I'll do a Bible study. But most times, the study is written by someone who has a certain agenda, and they want you to believe as they believe.

This is going to sound very gross, so I am going to apologize now. But, could you imagine going into a restaurant, ordering a delicious meal, it shows up and is sitting in front of you, and you ask the server, "Do me a favor, would you chew that up for me before I eat it?"

JL: [Laughing] Yes, it's gross, but I get it.

MG: Why would you let God speak to you through somebody else's filter? Let him speak to you personally, one on one. He wants to!

Much like he wanted to spend time with Jesus, he wants to spend time with us. Now, you ask what I say to someone who says they can't read the Bible in 90 days. I say: Of course you can. It takes about an hour a day. If you just commit to an hour a day, you can do it. Get up an hour earlier. Go to bed earlier so you can get up earlier. Maybe in the evening do a moratorium on TV. If you can't read in the morning, do it for an hour before bedtime.

For me, it works best to read the Bible in the morning, because what I get from reading gets me through the day. I need that meal first thing because that's the nutrition that's going to keep me from being hungry.

But the biggest point here is: You can't afford to not read the Bible. All throughout scriptural history, we read that the biggest problem with God's kids is that they did not spend time with him. They spent time with everything else, but they didn't spend time with him. They went through the motions—they did their sacrifices and rituals. Today, we say, hey, I go to church. I pay my tithe. I do this and this and this. That's wonderful, but are you spending time with God? Are you allowing him to chat with you?

Imagine being a parent and having kids that don't want to give you the time of day. It would absolutely break your heart. That's how God feels.

JL: One more thing that is off-topic, and then we will get back to the business focus. I hear what you're saying about Bible studies, and I hear what you're saying about reading the Bible, going to the source, but what about being in groups where you are reading and studying the Bible together?

MG: I don't think it's an either/or. I think it's both. I think there are benefits of getting together with others and studying and going deeper together, but that should never take the place of a quiet one-on-one relationship with God, where we can talk and listen. I mean, we often say, "God, speak to me about this."

JL: We often say that as we're running out the door or going into a meeting. How are we supposed to hear him then?

MG: Right! Let God speak to us through his Word. If it was good enough for Jesus, it should be good enough for us. [Laughing]

As an aside, when Paul was blinded for those three days, I believe that—much like the Father sat with the Son and said, "There you are, there you are," pointing to the places Jesus could learn about himself—Jesus sat with this rabbi, this Pharisee who had memorized scripture, and through the Holy Spirit, Jesus was saying, "Paul, here I am, here I am." And Paul got it. That's what changed him forever.

But back to your question: Getting together in groups is wonderful.

JL: Jesus wants us to be in a community.

MG: Absolutely. Look, Paul did that. You know, Paul had his quiet time, where he spent one-on-one with the Lord and in scriptures, and then he had his preaching, teaching time, too, where folks worked together.

Chapter Four

What are You
<u>Doing</u> Here?

Jacquelyn Lynn: Let's go back to the question: What are you doing here? What are you <u>doing</u> here? How do we figure out that <u>doing</u> element?

Mark Goldstein: We all are in business, doing something. But that isn't the reason we were put on this planet. It's the foundation to allow us to make money, to buy houses, food, cars—to live. But that's just the temporal, that's how you exist. The real reason we're here is to be in a relationship with others, to connect God and man through being who we are in what we do.

JL: Even so, God wants us to find satisfaction and meaning in our work.

MG: Yes. And we shouldn't spend our time in jobs that we don't enjoy. Think of it this way: How many churches are there? Too many to count. And in those churches are many, many styles of worship. We tend to go to churches where we feel like we fit, where we feel encouraged, excited, enthused, renewed, passionate—all of that. That's the way it is with jobs. We should choose work that excites us, that we are passionate about.

We shouldn't choose a career because somebody else said we should do that or because it's expected of us. If you grew up in West Virginia, it doesn't mean you should be a coal miner. You can be anything you want. You don't have to be a doctor because one of your parents was a doctor. Or an architect or a pastor. You should do what will make you happy, what will make you feel fulfilled, that will let you use the gifts God gave you.

My friend Kris DenBesten told me a story about being in a restaurant with a bunch of people and this guy was bussing and resetting the tables. He did it with such passion and enthusiasm that when he would start doing a table, everybody would stop eating and watch him, and when he finished, people would applaud. Kris says we should ask ourselves: Would anybody applaud if they were watching me do what I do for a living? Take it a step further—would Heaven applaud? We should be so enthusiastic about our work that Heaven would applaud our efforts.

JL: It makes sense that for work to be worship, we need to enjoy what we do. But is that all?

MG: I believe there's this thing—and I don't think you'll find it in any theology books—but I call it the nudge factor. I believe that all of us who are called by God, who have accepted that call, who are living our lives, even in our brokenness—we have a nudge gift. What is that? Well, imagine a continuum, a long line. At one end, there is a plus ten, and at the other end is a minus ten, and right in the middle is the cross.

-10 _____ +10

The plus tens would be Billy Graham, Bill Bright, Mother Teresa—people like that. The minus tens could be Adolph Hitler, Osama Bin Laden, and any other most evil, worst person you can think of.

That's the two ends, the two extremes. The rest of us are all somewhere in between on that continuum. Some people have accepted the Lord and are growing in grace, and they're either at plus one or up to plus nine. You have others who have not embraced the Lord and are anywhere from the minus one on down. So people are living their lives in whatever number on this continuum where they are.

Now, we all have this nudge gift, and we're specialists with our nudge gift. Maybe some people know their nudge gift, but I think most people don't. I think if we knew what our nudge gift was, it would be more about us and less about God. We would be thinking we are all that and a bag of chips, and it would be taking our eyes away from where they're needed.

But God knows the nudge gift—after all, he gave it to us—and he brings us into situations with people we can interact with and use our nudge gift to gently move them along the continuum, maybe from a minus seven to a minus six, or from a plus one to a plus two.

What might that look like? It may be that you have a killer smile and twinkle in your eye, and you're always finding yourself opening doors for people and saying, "Have a great day," and it makes a difference for them. Or you may have a gift where you just have a way of saying, "How are you?" and meaning it. You are constantly being brought into places where, through an interaction with someone, it gets them thinking. And maybe it nudges them from a minus six to a minus five. Then somebody else they interact with does something else through their special nudge gift, and it nudges them to a minus four. And so on.

Some people are blessed and honored with a gift that lets them help others either find the Lord or deepen their faith. And they often don't have any idea that's what they're doing. I know when I finally stepped across that threshold, I could look back and see God's fingerprints all along the way through different situations, with people he brought into my life. In retrospect, I could see it happening.

> "People want to work for a cause, not just for a living. When there is alignment between the cause of the firm and the cause of its people, move over—because there will be extraordinary performance."
>
> *William Pollard*
> *The Soul of the Firm*

Isn't that so God? With this incredible mosaic that he knows just where the tiles need to be and when they need to be there. He's not pushy, he just lovingly pulls us toward him and puts us where we need to be to do his work. Sometimes we know what that work is, often we don't. How many times have you heard stories about people who were feeling hopeless and depressed, who were thinking about committing suicide, and something happened. Someone spoke to them in a meaningful way. Someone did something for them, maybe as small as picking up something they dropped, but it made them feel that someone genuinely cared about them and maybe life is worth living after all. We don't know how often we use our nudge gift to do something that's small to us but incredibly meaningful to someone else.

JL: That's true. When we talk about gifts from God and our spiritual gifts, we tend to focus on major things. For example, I believe my ability to write is an absolute gift from God. Others might focus on their ability to teach, to heal, to cultivate and grow things—all gifts from God. But we don't talk about what you call the nudge gifts, the things that we probably do often without giving any meaningful thought to, without planning, and yet those actions can have such a tremendous impact.

MG: You are so right in that. As you are talking, I'm thinking that maybe we have overt gifts and covert gifts.

JL: Ah!

MG: A gift is something given to us by God that he uses to work through us. How much better could it be than for God to work through us without us realizing it? To me, that's just so God. But we have to be willing to let him use us. And we can spend our days doing all kinds of things and come home and say, "You know what? I did not see God doing anything overtly through me today, but it may have been one of the greatest Kingdom days in the history of humanity. I just don't know about it yet."

When people thank me for doing things, when I'm praised for something, I don't take credit for it. What I will take credit for is being obedient. Everything else is God. I've given God permission to work through me, and the only thing I can take credit for is obedience. The rest is him. It's an unbelievable privilege that even in my brokenness, even in my imperfection, he can do perfect things.

*JL: So, when Christians are in business, we have this under-
standing that we are to do things, function in a way, that demonstrates the integrity, the goodness of everything that our faith
teaches. But as big as that is, it may not be what God really has
in mind and what God is really doing through us. That could be
the nudges.*

MG: Absolutely.

JL: Or we could be on a double track and not realize it.

MG: I like the idea of a double track. There are things that
God calls us to do that help us grow and are for our benefit.
There are also things that God gives us the privilege of being
a part of that are for the benefit of others, and we don't know
that. So part of what God calls us to do, we can see. Part
remains unseen until sometime in the future. We are going to
have all of eternity to unpackage the amazing brilliance of
the work of God, the creativity of the Creator.

Chapter Five

What are You Doing <u>Here</u>?

Jacquelyn Lynn: Let's move on to the third part of the "What are you doing here?" question. What does the emphasis on <u>here</u> mean?

Mark Goldstein: The little hairs on the back of my neck always stand up when I hear somebody say, "I'm leaving business to go into ministry, and I'm going to go overseas." It's the idea that to go into ministry to do what God calls you to do means that you have to leave what you're doing and do something completely different in a place that's different. Some people think that's what ministry looks like.

In three of the four gospels, we read a story about Jesus going to Gerasenes. There are different takes on this in the three synoptic Gospels. Still, when you put it all together, Jesus goes across the Sea of Galilee, goes to Gerasenes, where he is met by a man who is demoniacally possessed by Legion because there were a lot of demons in him. Jesus cast the demons out of him, sent them into pigs, and the pigs jumped over a cliff into the sea and died. People showed up; they saw the guy who was formerly filled with Legion and heard about the pigs. They asked Jesus to leave because they were afraid.

Luke tells us the man who had been possessed asked to go with Jesus. Jesus told him to "stay here and tell your story." He must have done a good job telling his story because, when Jesus came back, we're told that everybody from the entire area came out to meet Jesus.

The point is: The man stayed home and told his story. The message for us is that we have to realize that our mission field starts right in our own home. It extends out into our front and back and side yards, to our immediate neighborhood, to our community, to our workplace, to—you name it. Our mission field is right in front of our eyes. We can be who we are, doing what God called us to do, right where he has called us to do it. We don't have to go anywhere.

Now, some people go to work for a particular ministry, and the ministry asks them to go overseas. That's not what I'm talking about. Ninety-nine percent of us are just fine right where we are. And God wants to use us right where we are.

> "He had been led to believe that business was of the world and that as he matured in his faith, Jeff would eventually be led to a higher calling, outside of business. Jeff recalls, 'In many ways it left me feeling guilt that as a businessman, I was a second-class Christian.' After much prayer and discussion with wise people, he discovered that his business was a higher calling and that it was his."
>
> *Larry Julian*
> *God is my CEO*

JL: *He wants us to grow where we're planted.*

MG: Exactly. Here's an example. When it comes to doing

God's work and our mission field, an organization's receptionist is just as impactful as the well-known evangelist or the corporate executive. But receptionists often don't get the recognition they deserve. They have just as much relevance, they have just as strong of a story, and they are as blessed gift-wise with the overt and covert gifts as anyone, anywhere. It's okay for us to say, "Lord, give me your eyes and ears, let me be the hands and feet to do what you've called me to do, *where* you've called me to do it."

JL: To summarize: We need to understand who we are, which is God's children and heirs; what we are supposed to do, which is to use the gifts God gave us; and where we are supposed to do it, which is God's plan for us.

MG: Right.

Chapter Six

How to Demonstrate Faith in the Marketplace

Jacquelyn Lynn: Let's talk about some of the ways we can demonstrate our faith in the marketplace without preaching.

Mark Goldstein: First and foremost is prayer. It's our honor, our privilege, and our duty to pray for others. It's selfish in a way because when we pray for others, it benefits us.

So who do we pray for? First, we have that hard-to-love person at work. They're hard to communicate with, they're irritating.

JL: I've heard those people described as EGRs—extra grace required.

MG: There you go. So we pray for them. Why?

JL: Good question. If we're a manager or we own the business, we could just fire them.

MG: But how can you pray for someone and then not want to engage with them in a better way? Praying for someone takes the edge off conflict. It puts the relationship at a different level. Sometimes it's hard to do, but we need to do it. When we pray for someone, what we're really saying is, "God, I would love for you to bestow on that person every grace, every mercy, every ounce of compassion that you put on me. I pray they have that, too. I pray they have a glimpse of eternity and the desire to be there. I pray all this and more for that person."

JL: *That sounds wonderful, but it isn't always easy to do.*

MG: It's not always easy, but if you do it, it's worth it.

Now, there is no doubt that God hears those prayers, and I believe he will answer them in a way that blesses you as well as the person you're praying for.

There's another aspect to praying for others that we should address. Churches often have prayer lists. In the Chamber, we share prayer requests. We find out about people who have problems, and we say, "Hey, let's get this on the prayer chain, let's get everybody praying." That's good, but I don't believe God sits in Heaven with a tally sheet. He's not watching, thinking that he needs 10,000 prayers to do this one, and we've only got 9,000 people praying. God doesn't work that way. He knows what we need, and he acts on it even before we ask.

So why should we respond to prayer requests? Why should we take the time to pray for someone we don't know? Or someone we have only the most casual relationship with? It's this: The more people who are praying for someone who has an issue, the more people are getting blessed themselves.

Let's say you're praying for someone who has cancer. Do we want the cancer to be healed? Sure. Will it be? Not always. Do we want that person to have all the good things that

God is willing and able to give? Yes. Will how God works be a mystery to us? Of course. Sometimes it's clear; sometimes it's not. And sometimes, part of the reason people go through challenges is to give other people the privilege and blessing of being able to grow themselves through prayer and service.

Now, bring that into the marketplace. When we are in a culture where Christians are praying for other people, yes, it's a blessing for the person getting prayed for. God is working in their life. People are nudging like crazy. But also, look at the growth, look at the blessing that comes to those who are praying.

So when we read that all things work together for good, that's the proof. There may be bad things, but good can come from it, not just for the person directly affected, but for anyone who has an interaction with that person.

That's a nuts and bolts foundational concept: If you are a Christian in the marketplace, first and foremost, you need to be a person of prayer—praying for yourself and also praying for others, regardless of who they are.

JL: Okay. What else can you do to demonstrate your faith in the workplace?

MG: There are so many ways, depending on your role in the business world.

Let's say you're in sales. What does that look like? First, you have a philosophy of serve, don't sell. You look at all the different ways you can help people instead of what you can get them to buy from you. We all love to buy; we all purchase things. But we don't like to be sold. So be a person who is a people helper, not just a sales rep. Under-promise and over-deliver. Exceed expectations. Provide outstanding follow-up, excellent customer service. That's what it means to be salt and light as a salesperson. It's taking all that honesty, that integrity, and letting it manifest in your interactions with people where your product or your service is just the catalyst for a relationship.

Let's say you attend networking events, either as a salesperson or a business owner or in another capacity. And by the way, I detest the word network as a verb.

JL: Networking, as an activity, is a part of doing business. Why don't you like using the word network as a verb?

MG: Because I find it artificial and disingenuous. When a person is networking and they see another person at an event, their first thought is, "Prospect! This is a potential customer. I'm going to approach them and find out quickly if they're a good prospect for my product or service."

The networking-as-a-verb mindset isn't focused on the person, it isn't focused on any kind of relationship. It's focused on a transaction. To me, that's like giving me a paper cut and pouring lemon juice on it. It's painful and a big waste of time.

JL: What do you recommend people do at networking events?

MG: Most people think of networking as going places to meet people to develop business. Right? You meet somebody at an event, and your agenda is to see if they have the potential to be your customer. That's probably their agenda, too. So you're both doing your expanded elevator speeches looking for ways that one of you might be able to sell to the other, and oftentimes there's simply no potential for you to do business.

So what do you do instead? Come into these events with the idea that you're not going to try to sell to anyone at all, but that you're coming to the table in servitude. You want to see how you can make the other person's life better, so you sit and you ask everything you can, not only about business but personally as well. You want to learn enough about the other person so you can feel comfortable recommending them.

We all love to recommend. When someone needs something, we all love to be able to say, "I know a guy" or "I know a lady." We recommend people because when that person shows up and exceeds expectations, it makes us look good. We're the heroes.

But we will only recommend people we trust, and we only trust people we know. We're not going to take a chance on burning relational collateral by recommending somebody who is going to disprove what we said, who is going to not show up or is going to do a lousy job. That makes us look bad.

So when you're meeting with people at events, you want to learn all about them. You want to get to know them, regardless of whether they're going to be your customer, because you want to know how you can recommend them to others. That's serving. It's building relationships, which builds business.

JL: In my previous professional life, before I began writing, I was in transportation sales and marketing. I've been through some topnotch sales training. One of the courses I took taught to ask questions so you can find out what the prospect needs, then you zero in with, "This is how we can meet your need, so buy from us." But what you're saying is, ask questions to find out who they are, what they do, and how they do it, so that you can go out and refer people to them.

MG: Not just refer. Recommend.

Referrals are great. If someone refers you, that will get

you in the door, but you still have to make the sale. A recommendation is much stronger. For example, a guy comes to me and says, "Hey, Mark, do you know a barber I can go to?" I might say, "Yeah, there's a barbershop in the shopping center I drive by every day. I don't know anything about it, but you could check it out." That's a referral.

But if the guy asks about a barber and my response is, "The best in the area is right up the street in that shopping center. His name is Phil. He's been cutting hair for years, he's been doing mine for ages, and you'll absolutely love him. You won't stop laughing. Make sure you ask him about the camel story."

That's a recommendation. You've put some skin in the game. So when you meet people, you don't just qualify them as prospects, you get to know them. You want to know enough so you can decide if you want to do business with them but also so you can recommend them to others.

> "Success in living a happy life is a larger project than success in business, and nearly everybody in business wants to achieve both."
>
> Michael Novak
> *Business as a Calling*

Zig Ziglar said it best: "You can have everything in life that you want if you help enough other people get what they want." So when you meet with somebody, find out how you can help them grow their business, irrespective of whether you can use their service because probably you can't, but over the next few months, you're likely to find a half dozen people who could and you can recommend them.

JL: Let's go back to comparing this approach to traditional sales training, where you qualify, pitch, and close. If I were taking a self-centered approach, I would be saying to you, "Mark, you're telling me to get out there and spend my time talking to people, finding out about them so that I can recommend them to other people. But I have to sell my product. When am I going to do that?"

MG: The magic of this is in that Zig Ziglar quote. When you help people, they can't help but want to help you. And it's not a quid pro quo, because if you're doing this, first of all, you are leading like Jesus. How many times do we read in the Gospel that he would ask somebody a question first? "What do you want?" In essence, how can I help you? He didn't force himself on anybody. He asked questions, so it was, "How can I help you? How can I serve you?"

It's the great disconnect from traditional selling. Because now the person you're talking with is going to know what they can do for you.

It's also realizing that not everybody is a customer. Not everybody will be a client. But everybody can be a raving fan. And that's what we're trying to do—we're trying to create raving fans for our business.

When Jesus departed, as we know, there were about 120 raving fans, and we met them all on the day of Pentecost. Jesus focused on the 120. We know there were 12, but we also know there were others and the 12 were the leaders—Jesus' inner circle, if you will. But Jesus spent time building a relationship with those 120. It wasn't quantity, it was quality. He spent time with people who got to know him and whom he got to know. On that day of Pentecost, he poured into them and they went out in one day, in one sitting, and grew into 3,000. Those 120 were raving fans through the relationship they had with Jesus. They spoke to others.

JL: *They were able and willing to do that because they were raving fans.*

MG: Exactly. People didn't see Jesus on that day. Who knows how many there were? But we know 3,000 said yes. They didn't see Jesus that day, they saw the 120 and heard Peter.

That's what raving fans can do for you. It's not finding one client; it's finding one raving fan because one raving fan will bring you many, many clients.

JL: *Raving fans will do your selling work for you.*

MG: Yes. I find it very easy to sell other people's stuff. I find it very difficult to sell my own stuff. I think we all have the ability to talk about somebody else with command, with authority, and with emotion. Oftentimes, when somebody hears a recommendation like that, they are sold. So when you've been recommended that way, all that's left to do is not blow the sale.

Jesus gave us a great example of what raving fans look like and the potential of having them.

As a salesperson, lead with your heart, lead with care, lead with "How can I help you?" Whatever business you're in, understand that being in business is the foundation of doing God's work, doing ministry. So as a salesperson sitting across from you, I know you may never be a customer, but you are somebody I can touch in some way, perhaps in a very tangible way. That's being salt and light. That's being that peculiar person Paul talks about in Titus.

JL: *Talk about how this works for people who are not in sales. They're in operations, finance, bookkeeping, administration, human resources. They're in all the support roles. They're not out* *there making sales calls. Their job doesn't depend on how many sales calls they make or how much revenue they generate. Their job depends upon doing the operations of the business or maybe just being the receptionist, answering the phone.*

MG: The 120 also illustrates this. They weren't rabbis. They weren't learned people. They were common folks. We've talked about how Jewish children memorize the Torah and the ones who excel at that are chosen to memorize the rest of the Bible. The ones who do a great job of that are chosen by the rabbis to follow them. In Jesus' time, if you didn't cut the mustard with the rabbis, you went back to your family business. Jesus chose people out of their family businesses, not out of the synagogues. These were all less than stellar students, but Jesus said, "Follow me," and they did. It was through that relationship that it all happened. But to your question about the people doing the work of the business—the 120 were ordinary people who did ordinary things. And they kept on doing their work while spreading the Gospel. Peter did not stop fishing. Paul kept making tents. But while they did those things, they talked and people listened.

JL: How do we take that lesson and apply it to the contemporary workplace?

MG: A lot of it has to do with Godly management. It's a trickle-down from the owner of the company, the head of the company, the whatever. They have to set the tone, set the standard.

I think the most important person in a company of any size that has people who call in or show up is the receptionist. Receptionists are the vice presidents of first impressions. When you call a company, often you decide whether or not you are going to do business with them in about the first five seconds of talking with the person who answered the phone.

When you show up at a place, it's that receptionist who sets the tone as to your whole perception of that company. Everybody in a company should know how important they are, how critical to the mission they are, and that knowledge comes from the top. That's part of Godly management.

Now, maybe you don't work for a Christian. Or you don't work for somebody who operates using solid Christian principles. You still have a responsibility and your job is still important. Let's say you're the bookkeeper. If you weren't doing the bookkeeping, would everybody else get paid? Or maybe you work in maintenance. If you weren't keeping the equipment in good working order, would the company still be able to produce whatever it makes?

Everybody in a company needs to realize what their mission is—their Godly mission and what they are doing for the company. We talked about salespeople, but what about the people in marketing? The people who create the ad campaigns and the promotions? They need to tell a truthful story. Don't spin, don't exaggerate. Develop a raving fan base built on the truth.

If you are in management, lead by the Golden Rule and stick with it. Study behavioral communication. I think every company, but especially Christian-owned companies, should have their employees do the DISC, which is the behavioral communication profile. It's more than just personality, it's how you communicate. Some people are very exacting, very detailed in their communication. Others are short and sweet. Some prefer to listen and not talk. Others tell stories and interact with people. There's a cute story that illustrates this. A kid asks his father what makes airplanes fly, and the father says, "I don't have time to tell you right now, so go ask your mother." And the kid responds, "Dad, I didn't want to know that much." [Laughing]

But seriously, you need to know what makes a person tick and how they communicate if you're going to communicate with them effectively. And often, you can alleviate conflict in a workplace just by knowing how people communicate and relate to others.

It's interesting to apply the DISC profile to the people in the Bible. The D is very direct, in your face. The I is interactive, the S is steady, and the C is calculating in a positive way because they want to know all the details so they can do an analysis.

In the Bible, Paul was a D. He was very direct. Peter was an I—interactive, impulsive, a ready-fire-aim guy. The apostle John was an S. He was very much about relationships, he was a counselor kind of person. Then Luke, the doctor, was a C. His gospel is longer than the others because he gives so much detail, wonderful detail. What would we have done without a C person, without Luke, to give us so much information and context?

If you are a person of faith living your faith, works are a byproduct of that faith. When you really know the you and you are in love with the you, and you are in love with the why and the what and the how of being you, you can't help but live your faith. We can't live two different lives. If you're a Christian in the marketplace, you'll bring in God's principles in a practical way. You don't have to say, "Hey, let's all get together and have a Bible study." You just live your faith in the day-to-day, mundane things you do, doing everything like you would do it for the Lord.

What is DISC?

The DISC assessment is a tool used for discussion of people's behavioral differences. It provides a common language people can use to understand themselves and others better.

What does DISC stand for? What do the letters mean?

There are different versions of the DISC profile developed by different people and organizations. The terms vary slightly, but the basic description is consistent.

Dominant, drive, direct

Confident, task-oriented, focused on accomplishing results, the bottom line

Behaviors

- Sees the big picture
- Accepts challenges
- Can be blunt
- Gets straight to the point

Influence, influential, inducement

Verbal and social; places emphasis on influencing or persuading others, openness, relationships

Behaviors

- Shows enthusiasm
- Likes to collaborate
- Is optimistic
- Dislikes being ignored

Steadiness, stability, submission

Passive, loyal, process-oriented; is cooperative, sincere, dependable

Behaviors

- Doesn't like to be rushed
- Calm approach
- Calm manner
- Supportive actions

Conscientious, compliant, careful, cautious, calculating

Analytical, precise, detail-oriented; focuses on quality and accuracy, expertise, competency

Behaviors

- Enjoys independence
- Wants the details
- Objective reasoning
- Fears being wrong

JL: When we say the word ministry, we might think of the big national and international ministries led by superstar evangelists, and that if we're going to share the Gospel, it's necessary to be up on stage and be a dynamic, articulate preacher. You're saying we can share the Gospel while we're living a normal life, while we're at work taking an order, sweeping the floor, or putting a widget in a hole.

MG: Absolutely. We've talked about Elijah. In 1 Kings 19, when Elijah was on Mount Horeb, God wasn't in the earthquake. He wasn't in the fire. He wasn't in all those big, big things. He was in that still, small voice.

JL: We've talked about the fact that it becomes instinctive to work with excellence and integrity when you're a person of faith who understands your <u>you</u>. Always wanting to do our best, to always do the right thing, is part of being in a relationship with God. But the reality is we don't always do our best. We don't always do the right thing, even when we know we should. Talk about that.

MG: One of the greatest things that John Crossman [founder of Crossman and Company, a commercial real estate firm, and Crossman Career Builders, a talent development organization], said at a Christian Chamber meeting was that Christians shouldn't do business with other Christians just because they are Christians. Christians—or for that matter, anybody—should do business with Christians because if they are Christians—and I would add Christians that understand the <u>you</u>—they're doing their business with excellence.

You've heard the popular C. S. Lewis quote, "Integrity is doing the right thing even when no one is watching." It's a good motto to live by. We can wear a façade; we can fool some of the people some of the time. But what it comes down to is that when we realize that work is worship, that what we're doing is honoring God, that what we do in the marketplace is as meaningful as standing in a pew, raising hands, singing a song, praying, listening to a sermon, interacting with people in church—that's worship. Being in the marketplace and having the privilege to nudge someone—that's a calling. That's worship, too.

JL: *It would be wonderful if everyone we're working with feels the same. But we have to be realistic and practical. We operate in a world that includes cultures that may not subscribe to our high standards. By cultures, I mean both in a broad, international sense and also in a narrow sense, as in the culture of a specific organization or company. So we may be dealing with people who aren't as ethical as we are or who don't mind cutting corners even if it means cutting quality. And if we're dealing internationally, we may, for example, be trying to operate in a country where bribery is the norm, but bribery is not only immoral, in the United States, it's also illegal. How do we integrate our Christian values with the real world?*

MG: Back in the day, several of my friends in the Air Force got stationed in the Philippines. If you wanted to get anything shipped out or if you want to pick up anything at the Port at Manilla, you had to grease some palms. And if you didn't do that, you lived with the consequences.

People have to make a choice. They can choose to acquiesce because of convenience or expediency. Or they can choose to draw a line in the sand and stand for righteousness.

We are salt and light. If we are a business owner, one of the wonderful things about being in charge is that we have a choice of how we conduct our business. And if we conduct our business with others who are not God-honoring, how is that going to look to our employees?

Going to the Bible, look at David and Bathsheba. David tried to hide what he'd done to Bathsheba and, when that didn't work, he had her husband Uriah murdered. There were issues with everything David did about that situation—issues within his family, within the army, and within the entire country because they saw what David had done. Was he forgiven? Yes. But were there repercussions? Absolutely.

If you own a company, or if you're in a management position with authority to make such decisions, and you capitulate to a supplier or a customer and do something contrary to your values, whether it's legal or not, there will be repercussions. Your employees will see it. It will reflect on you and on them. They may decide they don't want to work for a company that operates that way. Your suppliers and customers will find out. When they do, they may either ask you to go further down that negative slope, or they may decide they don't want to do business with you.

So, as a business owner or manager, what do you want your behavior to say about you?

Now, you may be in an industry and find that to survive in that industry, you have to do things that are against your principles. Then you have a decision to make. Do you stay, or do you go?

It's up to each individual—whether you're an owner, a manager, or an employee—to decide what to do based on your own conscience and relationship with the Lord. If you're an employee working for a company that you see is cutting corners, is less than truthful, or whatever, then you have to decide—are you going to capitulate to make money or are you in faith going to stand up for righteousness and God, and ask

God to get you someplace else?

God knows the end from the beginning. He knows our hearts. I think if we stay true to our hearts and true to our relationship with God, that's going to transcend where we go, what we do, who we work for, and who we align with. It can even help when you're getting ready to start a company. Ask yourself: "If I start this company, who will I have to interact with? What will I have to do to succeed?" Then decide if it makes sense for you even to go down that track. You may realize it doesn't.

JL: Give us some thoughts on operating with excellence and working with integrity when it comes to the relationships we have with our competitors.

MG: Too often, you see people in the same industry beating each other up.

JL: They see each other as the enemy.

MG: Yes, but the rising tide raises all ships. If we're doing what God has called us to do, we should not be afraid of competition. Competition is healthy. It can make us better. At the same time, you want to see your competitors doing well because it makes your industry do well.

> "Among a younger generation of Christians in business, working as financial analysts and engineers is itself Christian service. Their mindset is captured by Dave Evans, co-founder of the videogame giant Electronic Arts. Mr. Evans talks more like a theologian than a former Apple engineer. He points out that Genesis says that humans were created in the image of God, so all of our work—not just church work—is holy. We are called to be co-creators, with God, of a flourishing life on Earth."
>
> Rob Moll
> *Doing God's Work at the Office,*
> *The Wall Street Journal*

There are times when someone who is usually a competitor becomes an ally. I call it coopetition. For example, you may call on somebody, and they need something, but it's not really in your sweet spot. Or it might be one of those things that cause more work than it's worth. But you may have a competitor that is ideal for this customer. What does it say about you when you call a competitor and tell them, "I've got this prospect and they need this. I could do it, but I don't really want to because the project isn't right for us. Is this something you'd be comfortable doing? If so, I'll make the introduction." It says you want to do the right thing by your customers, your employees, and your company. It says you operate with integrity. And you know what else? It will come back to you. There will come a day when that competitor has a prospect that isn't in their wheelhouse, and they're going to call you.

JL: It may not come back from that competitor you gave the business to.

MG: It may not, but it will come from someone.

JL: But regardless of where it comes from, or if it comes at all, you taught the customer and the competitor a lesson.

MG: Exactly. You showed them how things ought to be done. Those of us who have been around longer than we might like to admit remember a time when members of the U.S. House of Representatives would argue heatedly on the floor of Congress during the day and at night would all go out and have steak dinners and drinks with each other. There was respect. There was a sense of unity. They understood they were all in it together. They might disagree, but they worked together.

Now, everybody demonizes each other. There's no relationship between them.

Bringing that closer to home, we have 56 chambers of commerce in Central Florida. The Christian Chamber is one of many. You could say that the other chambers are our competition. When people come to me asking if they should join this chamber or that chamber, I tell them to join the chamber or chambers that make sense for them. Of course, I want them all in the Christian Chamber, but I know that's not going to happen. And I know being in the Christian Chamber isn't always what's best for them. And even though the various chambers are competing for members, there are a number of them who work together holding joint events and activities for their members. It's a form of coopetition.

JL: I remember when members of Congress and other politicians could disagree graciously and still be friends. Before I became a full-time writer, I spent ten years in the transportation industry working for air freight and motor freight carriers. When I started, we were encouraged to be involved in transportation-related organizations. And if I had a customer who needed something my company couldn't do, I would refer them to someone I knew who could. And I got stars with the customer because I'd helped them. But then things changed. The carriers got concerned about price-fixing and antitrust and things like that, and we were told, "Be very careful that you are never seen in public having a one-on-one-conversation with a competitor." We were discouraged from making referrals. I was losing my network, and it was frustrating, but the companies were afraid of getting sued. So I know how tough it can be to operate in the real world the way you really want to.

MG: One of the things we have to remember is that God takes care of his kids. If he has called us to do something, he's not going to let us fail. He's going to let us get our fair share. In fact, oftentimes, because we are doing things the right way, the Godly way, without necessarily putting his name on it, we end up getting our unfair share. We not only get the share we should have gotten anyway, we also get the share of other people who aren't doing things that people can look at and say, "Hmmm" and think about the benefits of integrity.

That's another thing—in this time of social media, opinions and public comments can make or break you. What people say matters. It comes back to relationships. What kind of relationships are we building?

JL: And when it comes to social media and online reviews, it's just a fact that people are much, much quicker to criticize than to praise.

MG: Absolutely.

Chapter Seven

Serving Beyond the Mission of the Business

Jacquelyn Lynn: Let's talk about a business serving beyond the mission of the business. Some of that is going to be just the nature of the company's owners and leaders because they take personal joy in serving. But we often see businesses doing more. An accounting firm, for example, might have an official mission of "We help our clients plan a tax strategy and prepare their tax returns." Or a home builder's mission might be to build quality homes in a specific price range. But we see those businesses serving in other ways. We see the companies making donations of goods and services as well as cash. We see the employees participating in events like cleaning up parks or serving food to the homeless.

Mark Goldstein: A business owned and run by people of faith has multiple bottom lines. I'm sure there are more, but I look at a triple bottom line. In the Chamber, we talk about building business, building community, building Kingdom.

As a business owner, of course you want to make a profit. The first rule of business is to stay in business, and you do that by having a margin. You do it in all the right ways. You want to build your business, but when you do that, you understand that you may make the best widget in the world, you may sell more widgets around the world than any other widget-maker, and you're profitable, but that's not why God called you into business. That's not your end goal, it's just one bottom line.

The next bottom line is community, to build community. That's community within your company and community outside of your company. That's where getting involved, being a part of the positive footprint of the community—whatever that looks like and whatever piece God has called you to do—makes a difference. Get involved, do those good works that make that difference.

> "When humans act creatively, when we build things, make things, invent things, and imagine things, we are truly acting like God and using his power within us to the fullest."
>
> Anthony DeStefano
> *A Travel Guide to Heaven*

If you took every non-profit in Central Florida that engages in the social sector and pulled them out of the community, the social, economic, and spiritual landscape would change overnight. It would be disastrous. I'm sure that's true in most communities. Non-profits exist through the benevolence of people.

JL: *People who are making money.*

MG: Right. So by funding that engine, you are building community.

And the third bottom line is to build Kingdom. As much as we want to feed the hungry, clothe the naked, shelter the homeless, our ultimate desire should be to spend eternity with them. So that other bottom line is—

JL: *[using a mimicking tone] Oh, but they're dirty and they stink.*

MG: Yes, that's true. They did during Jesus's time and do now, too. But the leper came up to Jesus, and before Jesus healed him, he put his arms around him.

One of the things I love to do is serve at the Orlando Union Rescue Mission at Thanksgiving and Easter because I get to hug and be hugged by people where you can smell dying flesh. It reminds me of how blessed I am.

But the idea is that marketplace ministry means to be salt and light, to reflect the Kingdom, to be that catalyst that will draw people to us.

So as a business, it's that multiple bottom line. Not just to see how much money we can make.

Chapter 8

Choosing Your Associates

Jacquelyn Lynn: One of the most challenging things about the workplace and even life in general is other people. In our personal lives, we have a certain amount of control over who we associate with. If I don't trust someone, I can choose not to invite them into my home. We can keep some distance with neighbors if we feel like we need to.

But at work, in the marketplace, we have very little control over who we have to spend time with. We have to deal with a variety of personalities, sometimes toxic environments. Ask anybody—everybody has a "boss from hell" or "client from hell" story, probably way more than one. But sometimes we feel like we don't have a choice but to tolerate it. Maybe we need the job. Maybe there are so many things we like about the job that we're willing to overlook the difficult person or even the unethical thing the boss is doing. Or maybe we're the boss and we tolerate a toxic employee because they have a skill we need. What are your thoughts on how to deal with people we'd rather not be around?

Mark Goldstein: Wouldn't it be nice if we could just all get along? Like Rodney King said? That's utopia. It's not going to happen.

This is going to sound like it's coming from left field, but it works, so stay with me. The Bible talks about how we shouldn't divorce. But if a woman is married to a man and he is abusive and toxic, there is no mandate that says you need to stay in the relationship and be a punching bag. Get out. Any pastor who would say you should stick in there because the Bible says don't divorce ought to go to jail. Abuse is wrong, and Jesus doesn't want us to take it.

If you're in any kind of toxic, abusive relationship—personal or professional—and you've done everything you can do to fix it, and it's still not working, you need to get out of the relationship.

Let's say you're the owner or a manager of a company, and your people aren't getting along. You've had them all do the DISC profile to help everybody understand how to interact with people who communicate differently than they do. You've done everything else you can think of to do, but things are still toxic, you're losing sleep, it's affecting you physically, spiritually, emotionally. What can you do?

> "The work of Beethoven and the work of a charwoman become spiritual on precisely the same condition, that of being offered to God. This does not, of course, mean that it is for anyone a mere toss-up whether he should sweep floors or compose symphonies. We are members of one body, but different members with his own vocation."
>
> C.S. Lewis
> *The Weight of Glory*

Get out. Just get out.

Life is too short. If you've done everything you can do that is scripturally and ethically correct, and it isn't working, then for your own mental health, get out. If you're an employee, find another job. If you're a business owner, consider selling the company and doing something else.

We are just not called to be punching bags. We are not called to stay in situations and take it on the chin over and over again just to be some lesson for others.

There is a Jewish theology that I remember growing up with that the Jews deserved the Holocaust because of everything they did in the past, and that shows the world what happens when you disobey God. It was a lesson.

That's ridiculous! We don't need to get into the reasons the Holocaust happened, but it absolutely was *not* retribution from God for anything.

My point is that God wants us to have joy. He wants us to have joy in the morning, the afternoon, the evening. And if something is tearing us down and stealing our joy, and it's a situation we don't have to be in, move on.

JL: It's easy to say move on and get out. But you have people who may be trapped, or at least feel trapped. You have abused women who have kids and no money, nowhere to go. And in the workplace, you might have someone who doesn't have marketable skills, or maybe the job market for what they do is limited. Maybe this is the only employer. Any advice for the people who say, "I can't get out."

MG: I think some people can't, but God can. Sometimes we look at things horizontally. We need to be looking vertically. I know there are people in their late 40s and early 50s who have been with a company for a while, they're miserable, but they're sticking it out because they feel like if they quit, they'll be unemployable because of their age.

God has a thousand ways of meeting our needs, most of which we don't even know. I don't think there are ever impossible situations, but there are situations that look bleak. Having a circle of friends, of mentors, of colleagues, of folks you can call on to pray with you and to seek counsel with will help you get through these difficult situations.

JL: I have known people who are in bad situations, they say they want help, but they reject every possible solution you offer.

MG: Some people like to wallow in their pain. There are a lot of reasons for that. In some cases, it's because through their pain, they get attention, and through the attention, they get relationships. And that circles back to how important relationships are. But, regardless of the reason, some people get a lot of comfort in their pain.

JL: But God doesn't want us to be in pain.

MG: No, not at all. One of the best ways to deal with pain and problems is through work. Work is redemptive. To be able to have something to do with our hands—even in the very beginning, Adam had a job: Name the animals and tend the garden. That was his work.

Go back to David. The source of David's problems came when it was spring, the time when kings go off to war, but David stayed home. Joab and the army went to fight the Ammonites. David was at home and he got up one night, and from the roof of his palace, he saw Bathsheba bathing. We know how that played out. But the point is, what got him in trouble was not doing what kings did back then. He didn't go off to war. He didn't do his work.

As I've said, work is redemptive. Coming back to work

as worship, work connects us with God in the marketplace to where we can see him working, oftentimes in miraculous ways—answering prayers, giving us the opportunity to praise him. It also gives us the blessing of being able to earn a living so we can be good spouses, parents, stewards.

That's what it comes down to: Work as worship allows us to be stewards. People don't own their companies. When you stop and think about it, they are stewards. Everything we have belongs to God.

Back during the time of the Old Testament, people did not really own their property. God owned it. That's why they couldn't sell it. It came back in the jubilee because it was God's. It wasn't the individuals' property.

I'll give you a personal example. I was president of the Christian Chamber for about eleven years. The Chamber is a 501(c)(6). That means it's a nonprofit, but there is no owner-ship of it. When I left the Chamber, I didn't take anything, any kind of money or profits. I was a steward of the Chamber. The Chamber belongs to the members—really, it's God's Chamber.

I think that's the way we ought to look at for-profit busi-nesses. They grow because we stay in connection with God. Now, do non-Christians have very successful businesses?

JL: Of course. You don't have to be a Christian to be a good businessperson.

MG: Absolutely. But what it all comes down to in the end—I always say the difference between Bill Gates and me is that his ash pile is going to be much bigger than mine. We defi-nitely do not take it with us.

JL: Everything we have belongs to God. We're only taking care of it for him while we're here, and then it passes to another steward.

MG: Right. What's important is not that we build barns and more barns to fill up with stuff. It's what we're *doing* here and now—and that's what makes work worship. It keeps us in connection with God in an amazing and yet very practical relationship.

We see that in action among Chamber members all the time. For example, we had a member who was dealing with a challenging legal situation. She couldn't afford a lawyer, so she was going to try to handle it in court herself. She asked for prayers. Another Chamber member is an attorney who offered to represent her at a reduced rate. And a group of other Chamber members—some who barely knew her—chipped in to pay the lawyer's fee. Sure, they prayed for her, but they also took action. And they didn't do it expecting anything in return—it was an act of worship.

Here's another Chamber example: The members were a couple who owned a small business. The wife was pregnant—it was a high-risk pregnancy, so all of a sudden, she couldn't work in the business, she couldn't do anything at home, they weren't ready for the baby. When Chamber members found out, they scheduled a work day. About 20 people spent the entire day at this couple's home, cleaning, organizing, assembling furniture, getting the nursery ready. When the husband got home and saw what had been done, he was overwhelmed. People from all walks of life dropped what they were doing for a day to focus on this couple's needs. And while they worked together, they got to know each other in a way they hadn't before. Remember we talked about raving fans? Those people are now raving fans of each other—and it was all through an act of worship, an act of Godly service.

Chapter Nine

Fighting the Demons

Jacquelyn Lynn: Whether we're in business or school or running a household or whatever, there are times when we get buried in "stuff" and it suffocates us. When that happens, we're tempted to give up—and sometimes we do.

Mark Goldstein: This goes back to knowing our <u>you</u>, knowing who we are. When we are looking at the horizontal versus the vertical, "stuff" happens. If we don't have that <u>you</u> thing going on that lets us keep things in perspective because we know who we are in God's eyes regardless of what's happening that day, it's easy to start focusing on the weight of the world and let it bury us.

When you wake up at three o'clock in the morning and it's dark, the problem that woke you up always seems worse than when you wake up and can look at things in the bright light of day. And it's a natural human tendency to try to do it on our own, but that's when we start just filling in the squares and going through the motions.

The adversary is a pretty good psychologist. And he hits

us all the time. There isn't a day that goes by where he isn't attacking us with something. He knows when we are having a relationship with God. He doesn't know what we're talking about, but he knows when we're having relationship time and when we're not. And he knows that when we're not, it's easy to pile on and pile on. It's like in the ring when a boxer thinks he has stunned his opponent, he's going in for the kill. It happens when a shark smells blood. It's the same thing—the adversary knows when to attack. He knows when to hit us, he knows when we're at our most vulnerable.

JL: *What do we do when that happens?*

MG: We need to be prepared. We need to stock up, to fill up in advance, and then feed ourselves regularly. We need to have relationships. We need our go-to people—the people we can be real and vulnerable with, who don't think any less of us for sharing.

> "What amazes you seems quite natural to me: God has sought you out right in the middle of your work. That is how he sought the first, Peter and Andrew, John and James, beside their nets, and Matthew, sitting in the customhouse."
>
> *Josemaria Escriva*
> *The Way*

If we decided that for the next ten days, we're not going to eat or drink anything, we'd be hurting—we might end up in the hospital, we might even die. That's what happens when we don't take in spiritual nourishment. Our <u>you</u> atrophies and we become vulnerable. We can prevent becoming vulnerable with spiritual nourishment that comes with reading the Bible, talking with God, being a part of a community of believers, intentionally building the Kingdom.

Knowing our you doesn't mean that we're not going to have issues. It doesn't mean we're not going to fall. It means that we're never going to break. We might bend, but we're not going to break.

So to keep from breaking, we need to stay in the game—and the game is that whole relationship with God and with our community and realizing where you are supposed to be. It's also understanding that we are not in a utopia. Sometimes there won't be a good answer, and we have to accept that.

JL: One of the ways the demons, as I call them, get to us is through comparison. We look at others who might be better off financially or socially. We compare ourselves to people who look more successful than we are.

MG: It's so easy to compare. It's so easy to start questioning why someone has something and you don't. And it sounds trite just to say you should count your own blessings. Certainly, that's part of it, but to find peace, take it deeper. Learn your strengths and weaknesses. Look at what God has specifically gifted you with, what your uniqueness is. And remember that as God's children, as God's heirs, we have the same inheritance coming to us as the celebrity who lives in a multimillion-dollar home that's going to be as much rubble as your smaller house eventually. Keep that perspective and remember what being a child of God really means to you and the people you are around.

JL: But you're not saying that the common goal of Christians should be to exist in poverty, live in shacks, and drive beat-up cars.

MG: Of course not. It's like vanilla. When a recipe calls for vanilla, you can under-vanilla and you can over-vanilla. And as nice as vanilla is, you can really mess up the recipe if you don't use the right amount.

There is a narrow road, and it's easy to fall to the left or fall to the right—and I'm not talking politically. There are those who will say, "Oh, God called me to live in destitution. He called me not to have much because he needs to use me as a lesson for others." While that might be true, it could also be an excuse for being lazy, not having goals, not being assertive. Of course, there are people who live by faith and they travel there.

JL: Like Mother Teresa.

MG: Yes. But those people know their dependence came from God. They know we are not called to just die of starvation.

So you have people on one end who are very much practicing destitute theology, and you have people on the other end that are preaching and living prosperity theology—they name it and claim it that God wants me to live in a multimillion-dollar house, drive expensive cars, and so on. The thing is, they may have a ton of stuff, but that doesn't mean it's because God has lavished them with money and material things. That idea gets scary because people who don't have a lot of stuff start to think they're not good enough or worthy enough or whatever.

The answer is in the middle. God wants us to operate out of prosperity, not scarcity.

When you are on an airplane and the altitude changes and the oxygen masks come down, what are you supposed to do?

JL: Put your mask on first, then help people around you.

MG: Right. You stabilize yourself, then you put the mask on your child or whoever else needs help.

You can't minister to others when you don't have anything yourself. If you're needier than the people you're trying to help, you can't be effective. It's not a good witness.

God wants us to be effective in marketplace ministry. There's a balance, and Solomon talks about it—not too much, not too little, temperance in all things. God gives us what we need when we need it. I think you find that the Christians who are making bucket loads of money are giving bucket loads of money. People who are doing things that are honoring to God are reflecting what their relationship with God looks like.

Chapter Ten

How Workplace Worship Relates to Church

Jacquelyn Lynn: How does workplace worship relate to the church? By church, I mean the organized contemporary entity that we understand as the structure through which we practice our faith, not the Church of Biblical times.

Mark Goldstein: Both have their places, and this is where we need more collaboration. If you ask the average pastor, most will admit they really don't understand business and business-people. And they don't know how to equip businesspeople in the marketplace.

Pastors of churches know how to do church and, for the most part, they do a good job. If they don't, people stop going there and the church closes up. So churches that are staying healthy and thriving financially and in other ways are meeting the needs of the people at that time. For whatever reason, people are going to church. It's there for them, and that's wonderful.

But it's marketplace ministry—the business community—that connects Sunday to Sunday. It allows you to apply all the theoretical, all the theological information you are learning at church. You get to apply that in environments that are sometimes unsafe. You really get the acid test. You get to see if your faith truly is your faith—if you're a contender or a pretender. You're going to know very quickly if it all holds water. If your faith cannot be applied, it's not faith. It has to go from head to heart to hands and outward. That's what marketplace ministry allows. That's what being in business allows. That's why you can worship on Sunday or whatever day you worship, and you can continue to worship in a different venue throughout the week because of all the things you are taking from that worship service.

Should churches be more engaged with businesses, with marketplace ministry? Some are doing it, some aren't. Could it be better? Yes. With the Christian Chamber, we're not trying to take the place of a church, we're complementing the church. We want to work in partnership with churches to apply the message of the Gospel and strengthen our relationship with God.

> "All labor that uplifts humanity has dignity and importance and should be undertaken with painstaking excellence."
>
> Martin Luther King, Jr.

Here's an illustration. Those who ride motorcycles will know what I'm talking about. You buy a brand new battery, put it in your motorcycle, and leave the motorcycle parked for three weeks. Then you decide it's time to go riding. But the engine won't start because the battery is dead. It's a brand new battery, but it's dead. It dies from non-use.

You can go to church and fill your battery up to the brim but if you don't use it, if you don't engage in everything you know and everything God will bless you to do during the week, your battery is going to die.

It all starts with knowing who you are, understanding the you, being in a relationship with God, using the gifts you have to be a blessing. It's also understanding that there's a "nudge" you that is exciting beyond comprehension. You don't have to go to Bangladesh to be useful to God.

JL: If you were counseling a pastor of a church, what advice would you give them on how to minister to businesspeople?

MG: Great question. And the answer is to ask questions. Jesus was a great questioner. He asked great questions. My advice to pastors is to engage with your businesspeople. Ask them:

- What is your business challenge in the marketplace?
- What are your fears?
- What wakes you up at three o'clock in the morning?
- How are you dealing with those challenging people?
- How do you love the unlovely?
- How do you determine how much you're going to pay people?
- How do you balance your profits?
- How do you determine where you are going to draw the line as to what are acceptable business practices?

Find out what they need and speak to that. Work with them on it. Create business groups in the church. Spend time with your businesspeople at their workplaces. If they own a restaurant, spend a day there working in the kitchen, serving tables, working the cash register, whatever. If they have an insurance agency, spend some time in their office learning what they do. If it's a printer, go there and learn what some of the challenges are. Get to know them in their work environment so you understand what they need.

Back in the day when I sold radio advertising, I would

spend a day at each one of my advertisers to learn exactly what they did. It helped me in creating the right radio ads for them. If pastors would do that with their businesspeople, it would help create a relationship where the pastor can sincerely help the businessperson, and the businessperson will become more involved in the church.

Pastors need to put on a business hat and say, "Okay, what are some of the practical, tangible needs of businesspeople?" and speak to that. Maybe once a month preach business-related, nuts and bolts, practical sermons on dealing with whatever they've identified as an important issue. That's one way pastors can serve the businesspeople in their congregations.

JL: I'm sure some pastors do that, but I've never known one.

MG: I think pastors are often intimidated by businesspeople; they are kind of afraid of them. Because businesspeople are often substantial givers, pastors are beholden to them to pay their salary, so the pastors don't want to tick off any of their businesspeople members. But pastors don't really understand what being in business nowadays looks like. A great book every pastor who wants to understand how to help business-people should read is *The Shine Factor* by Kris DenBesten. Shine is an acronym:

Serve others
Honor God
Invest in eternity
Navigate with values, and
Excel in relationships.

As a counselor, if you ask good questions, you're going to get enlightening answers. But pastors often see their businesspeople as the budget-makers. They are the ones who keep the finances in the church. They are the ones who stay active. They are the deacons, the elders—whatever leaders are called in the congregation.

The way pastors can serve those businesspeople is by helping to equip them, to empower them to take the theological and make it practical, to encourage and support them in the marketplace. When that happens, it's good for the business person, it's good for their company, and it's good for the church. Those people who are engaging in the marketplace are out there meeting people, and people who are drawn to them will inevitably ask them where they go to church.

That's a perfect opportunity for businesspeople to invite other people to church. But there's that whole recommendation thing we talked about—are they going to look good when someone they invite comes to your church? Are the guests going to get something relevant when they come to your church?

That's where a pastor's collaboration and partnership with members of the congregation who are in business comes in. Where you might have had a hundred raving fans out there before, now that your messages can be applied in the marketplace, you can grow that to a thousand or more raving fans. To be clear, it's not either/or. It's not preach only business-related messages or preach only non-business-related messages. It's both. You need both.

Businesspeople in the marketplace have the potential to have more impact in any given week than a pastor has in a year. Pastors need to recognize that and work with it.

Remember the illustration of the continuum I used when I was explaining the nudge factor? As far as interacting with either non-Christians or Christians on that nudge scale, most pastors are regularly dealing with the plus ones and upward. The rest of us, more often than not, are interacting with minus ones on down. So just by mere availability and geography, we're meeting with more people and have the opportunity to let our faith have an impact on more people.

> "In addition to ignoring the issues faced by businesspeople, seminaries offer little analysis of or appreciation for the moral roots of modern corporation, the concept of business as a calling, or multiple tasks that business performs for society and the common good."
>
> David W. Miller
> God at Work:
> The History and Promise of the
> Faith at Work Movement

JL: *Because pastors, when they're not preaching, are usually spending most of their time operating the church and doing things around other Christians.*

MG: Right.

JL: *And when businesspeople head out into the marketplace, who knows what they're going to be dealing with?*

MG: Exactly. And let's be honest: We all tend to put on that church persona, that church façade. We say certain things, we do certain things when we're at church for weekly worship, when we encounter our pastor in the grocery store, when we come to a church function during the week. It's just natural. So even when pastors are interacting with their church people outside of church, they're still getting the church persona. And when we're dealing with people who need what we have to share, we'll be more effective if we take off that church persona.

JL: *Related to the issue of how workplace worship relates to church is how businesspeople can contribute to their churches* *through their business acumen. Is that another way we can build the Kingdom?*

MG: Absolutely. When you talk to people who run nonprofits, they say, "No margin, no ministry." They can't operate, they can't do their ministry without money. Oftentimes in churches, the biggest challenge is financial—hitting the budget. There are business practices that can be brought into churches to help them run more efficiently and do their ministries more effectively. Business leaders can be a blessing to pastors in more ways than by giving money and serving as deacons and elders. They can give good, practical help.

Chapter Eleven

The Blessing of Seeing the Fruit We Sow

Jacquelyn Lynn: We live and work in a culture that many people of faith find challenging. The divisiveness in the political arena, the animosity between various groups, and the strong feelings many people have—positive and negative—about different faiths all contribute to an environment in which some people might find it easier just to leave their faith at the door when they go to work. What would you say to those people?

Mark Goldstein: You can't do anything without faith—not necessarily religious faith, but faith in something. Everybody has faith in something. It's just what you decide to put your faith in.

As Christians, we cannot live our lives and not have faith.

Christianity is not about religion. It's about relationships. As human beings, we can't live our lives void of relationships.

Unfortunately, we live in a world where there is a lot of fear. People are afraid of everything. And because of that, they are afraid to embrace anything.

If you believe in something a little different, then it's

automatically wrong to some people. Because it's not in my box, it's not in my little wheelhouse of what I'm comfortable with.

We like to be comfortable. Anytime you try to get people out of their comfort zone, to stretch them, they are usually going to resist.

JL: So are you saying it's the Christians who are going to resist or just people in general wherever you happen to be?

MG: Both. Look at denominations these days. Christians will go to war with each other because one doesn't believe you should speak in tongues and the other doesn't believe you should *not* speak in tongues. Or one doesn't believe you should use any Bible other than the King James. Or doesn't believe you should come to church in jeans and an untucked shirt. Or that you should pray without kneeling. Or that you should have a drum and electric guitar in the church.

Over and over, people of faith go to war against other people of faith because one doesn't believe like the other. That's one way Christians resist getting out of their comfort zones.

But it's not just Christians. Often between Christians and non-Christians, it becomes a "them" and "us." The non-Christians say, "I'm not going to hang around Christians because they have an agenda. They're going to try and get me to come to their church." While we Christians don't want to hang around non-Christians because "oh, my goodness, I could get their cooties." [Laughing]

You see the fear, the resistance to change, the suspicion of different opinions on both sides.

JL: You've had a varied career—advertising sales, your own marketing company, president of the Christian Chamber of Com-

merce, area director of Christian Leadership Concepts. Of course, what I'm going to ask doesn't apply when you're working within Christian organizations, but you still do marketing consulting. Do you or did you ever feel like you have to hide your faith?

MG: I have never been shy about showing my faith. I've never felt a need or desire to hide my faith. I am who I am, and my faith drives what I do, why I do it, how I do it, and to hide from it and explain it some other way would be disingenuous. Now, did I ever lose business because of my faith? Sure. But if I had hidden my faith or just downplayed it and taken that job or that client, I would have been miserable. I would have felt like I couldn't be myself with that client. It isn't just the job you do, it's who you do it with. It's the potential of being salt and light in their lives. If I had to hide who I am, I might miss the whole reason for even working with them.

Here's an example: I was working with a client and went into their office one day. I call a company's receptionist the minister of first impressions because they are often a person's first impression of the business. That day, the receptionist at this client's office was not her typical wonderful minister of first impressions. You could tell there was an issue. I asked her if everything was okay, and she hedged and said yes, but you could tell she was just putting on a brave face. So I asked again and she shared something that was going on. I was able to give her a resource to help with the situation, but more importantly, I stopped what I was doing and we prayed. I prayed out loud for her right then. I went on to take care of the business I was there to do, and before I left, she told me, "Thank you, Mark. The problem isn't solved, but I feel so much better. I feel so much more at peace than before you came in."

That may have been the only reason I got that client, the only reason why they contracted with me, because of that moment I was going to be with her. If you are working with a client and you have to hide your faith—no, I can't. So, will I lose business? Sure. But I'll gain so much more.

In the Christian Chamber, we have fewer major sponsors than most any other secular chamber. It's because some companies do not want to risk offending their customers, clients, vendors, and employees by attaching their name to the Christian Chamber—which I find ironic, even if some are supposedly Christian-owned. It's crazy that way. But would I change anything in the Chamber to make it so others could come in? No. Because then, who are we? We would be just like any other chamber without a God uniqueness to it.

> "God give me work, till my life shall end and life, till my work is done."
> *Epitaph of Winifred Holtby*

JL: And if you choose to work with people from whom you have to hide your faith, sooner or later, your faith is likely to be challenged or compromised.

MG: Absolutely. If you swim with the sharks, you become a shark. You have to if you're going to survive. Also, if you can't be yourself, then whatever you're doing as work becomes drudgery.

You hear people say, "I need to be salt and light, so I have to go in very carefully and then let my life be the silent witness." That sounds good on paper—it sounds *real* good on paper. But if you go in without a strong statement of who you are—I'm not saying go in wearing a big cross around your neck, I'm saying don't shy away from showing your faith—

people can get the wrong impression, and then what have you accomplished?

JL: If you get intentional about it, there are so many ways we, as Christians, can plant seeds in the marketplace.

MG: Yes. We are not pastors, we are not paid clergy or even paid church staff. We are plumbers, architects, doctors, construction workers, merchants, authors, artists—we are all these things, operating in our respective business arenas, and sometimes it's easy to think that even though we work hard, we don't preach sermons or share messages and therefore don't bring people to Christ. That's not true. As marketplace ministers, we have a unique ability to plant seeds and see the fruit, to see in both tangible and spiritual ways how God has used us. Sometimes it's what we do, sometimes it's relationships and connecting other people. In my role with the Chamber, I saw it every day—story after story of things that have happened because of relationships in the marketplace. And when you see these things happening, when you see the fruit, it reminds us over and over again, that God is faithful, that he is the same yesterday, today, and tomorrow.

JL: Do you have any final thoughts you'd like to share?

MG: Along with work is rest. After six days, God rested. Now, the concept of God resting may seem a little weird, but if we look at it as an example for us—he made all this wonderful stuff and then he took time to enjoy it. He took time to reflect on it. So work is worship, but so is rest. We worship just as much when we rest as when we're working.

JL: Good point. I wrote a blog about that, it's on my website. It

*says that we are made in the image of God. God worked and God
rested. And that's what we're supposed to do.*

MG: Exactly. You can only go and do so much and then you
have to take a break, or your effectiveness declines. God knows
that, Jesus knew that. If we don't take some time for rest and
restoration, to enjoy the fruits of our labor, then it's really
all for naught. We don't have to work twenty-four hours a
day, seven days a week. If we're working in God's company,
enough will get done in the time he wants us to allocate for
work, as long as we are using sound Biblical principles.

Chick-fil-A is a great example. Back when it started going
into malls, if you were in a mall, you had to be open when the
mall was open, and most malls are open seven days a week.
Mall tenants pay a percentage of their gross revenue as part
of their rent. So mall operators figure if a store isn't open,
they're losing money. But Chick-fil-A is closed on Sunday, and
they challenged the mall operators to let them prove what
they would do. And they would consistently do more business
in six days than the other businesses would do in seven.

Another example is a locally owned restaurant chain,
4 Rivers Smokehouse, which is the flagship of the 4R
Restaurant Group. They're growing, they do an incredible
business, and they close on Sunday. I think it comes down to
rest—God honors rest.

JL: Anything else?

MG: Going back to talking about purpose and people trying to
figure out how to define "my purpose." It's the "What are you
doing here?" in every way. It's not linear, it's multi-dimen-
sional. In business, we'll have weeks that perhaps the profit
and loss statement didn't look too good, but we cherish that

week because of a relationship that was created, or a problem that was solved, or a service that was done. It may be that your best client of the year was one that you lost money on, but you were able to do something life-changing for them.

Success isn't defined by just what we are able to see. Success is defined by so much more, and some of that we won't see while we're still vertical and taking breaths. Some things have eternal consequences, and we may be just one tiny tile that goes into this future mosaic.

In Hebrews 11, we get the champions of faith—Abel, Enoch, Noah, Abraham, Sarah, Isaac, and so many others. They did things by faith. They didn't see the results that we get to see, looking back in history, yet they did all of what they did by faith.

Look at Paul in 2 Corinthians 11, where he writes about so much that happened to him. He dealt with it on faith. He didn't get to see the results of the body of work that he wrote, the lives his words have touched, and what happened generationally after he died. He didn't get to see any of that, but he had faith.

We need to not have myopic vision. Don't be overly excited about the good stuff, and don't be overly discouraged about the bad. Just answer the "What are you doing here?" question on all three dimensions and let that guide you. And realize that in marketplace ministry, the rules are a little different and the math isn't exactly what the world would say math should be. In marketplace ministry, our ultimate boss is not a boss. He is a loving guide.

JL: It all comes from relationships, but it all starts with our relationship with God.

MG: Absolutely. That's work as worship. Worship is a very intimate, personal relationship. In essence, we understand and embrace who God is, and we know who we are. We love this beautiful dynamic that just blows us away. Then, to be able to express it in very practical, meaningful ways in the marketplace with coworkers, employers, and employees, vendors, and so on—that's where faith shines. And that's where salt and light happens through very peculiar people.

Thanks to In the Company of Prayer [companyofprayer.com] for sharing many of the quotes used as callouts in this book.

A Gift from Mark Goldstein

How to Relationally Work a Room

Get Mark's advice before you go to your next networking event. Download your copy now:

CreateTeachInspire.com/markg

About Mark Goldstein

Mark Goldstein is the past president & CEO of the Central Florida Christian Chamber of Commerce, president of On The Mark Consulting LLC, and the area director for Christian Leadership Concepts. Mark is best described as a "people helper." He has an intense passion to help others succeed in business and ministry by developing and implementing creative marketing strategies. His more than thirty years of experience in sales and marketing includes broadcast media, print, home-based, internet, and trade show.

Mark holds a bachelor's degree in theology and a master's degree in Christian counseling. He is currently completing a doctorate in the same field of study.

With the Christian Chamber, Mark's goal was and continues to be to build business, build community, and build the Kingdom. As president of On The Mark Consulting, he helps individuals and businesses enhance communication and grow through relational marketing. As area director for Christian Leadership Concepts, Mark equips groups of men to be leaders, based on a growing, vibrant relationship with Jesus Christ and dedication to sound biblical principles.

About Jacquelyn Lynn

JACQUELYN LYNN finds joy in her faith, family and friends, as well as in the knowledge that she is living God's purpose for her life. She is an independent publisher, publishing consultant, and the author or ghostwriter of more than 40 books, including the Conversations series; *The Simple Facts About Self-Publishing: What indie publishers need to know to produce a great book*; *Choices*, the first novel in the Joyful Cup Story series; *Finding Joy in the Morning: You can make it through the night*; and *Words to Work By: 31 devotions for the workplace based on the book of Proverbs*. She is also the co-creator of a series of Christian coloring books for adults. For a complete list of books by Jacquelyn Lynn, go to **CreateTeachInspire.com/our-books**.

Visit **CreateTeachInspire.com** to connect with Jacquelyn. There you'll find links to join her email list and engage with her on social media.

A Gift from Jacquelyn Lynn

Get your free copy of

The Mindset of High Achievers:
What it takes to get what you want

Download your copy now at:
CreateTeachInspire.com/mindset

Conversations

Experts share their knowledge and experience

Titles in the Conversations series include:

For a complete list of titles and expert sources with links to order, visit createteachinspire.com/conversations.

To suggest a topic for a Conversations book, send us a message at CreateTeachInspire.com/contact.

What does it take to publish a quality book that will delight your audience and meet your goals?

The Simple Facts About Self-Publishing: What indie publishers need to know to produce a great book explains:

- The three primary paths to publishing and how to choose the one that will work best for you
- The most common mistakes self-publishers make and how to avoid them
- How to produce a book that will look as good or better than the ones from top traditional publishers
- How to identify and protect your book
- How to find the best service providers to help you write, produce, and publish your book
- What resources are available to support indie publishers and how to find them
- How to use your book as a marketing tool
- And much more!

  Available on Amazon and wherever books are sold.

A single moment
The wrong choice
Lives change ...
forever.

Available on Amazon and wherever books are sold.

Get through life's darkest nights
and find joy every morning

Available on Amazon and wherever books are sold.

Use the *Finding Joy Journal* to help you keep track of
what brings you joy, let go of what doesn't, and guide
you along your own joyful journey.

Available on Amazon and wherever books are sold.

Messages of inspiration and motivation based on the teachings of the world's greatest business advisor: King Solomon.

Devotions ideal for beginning your work day, opening a meeting, or just taking a break.

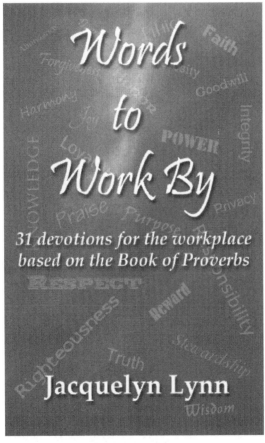

Available on Amazon.

Color Your Faith!

Available on Amazon.

Made in the USA
Columbia, SC
11 June 2020